GENERAL CONDITIONS
OF GOVERNMENT CONTRACTS
FOR BUILDING,
CIVIL ENGINEERING,
MECHANICAL AND ELECTRICAL
SMALL WORKS

C1001

Department of the Environment

Property Services Agency

Her Majesty's Stationery Office

© Crown copyright 1985
First published 1983
Second edition 1985
ISBN 0 11 671507 3

CONTENTS

Various words and phrases used in the Contract are defined in the Glossary at the end of these Conditions. Defined words and phrases are highlighted in the Conditions by initial capital letters.

1
Assignment and sub-letting

The Contractor must not:

(a) assign or transfer the Contract or any part, share or interest in it without the Authority's written permission; or

(b) sub-let any part of it without the SO's written permission.

2
Execution of the Works

(1) The Contractor must:

(a) commence the Works when told to do so in the SO's written order for work to proceed; and

(b) complete them, in accordance with the Contract and to the SO's satisfaction, on or before the Date for Completion.

(2) The Contractor must provide all Things necessary for the execution of the Works, except where the Contract specifically says otherwise.

(3) The SO may at any time order the Contractor to replace, repair, reconstruct or remove any part of the Works or any Thing for Incorporation which, in the SO's opinion, is not in accordance with the Contract; and the Contractor must promptly comply with the SO's order at his own cost.

(4) The Contractor must, if required, deliver the Specification(s) and/or the Drawing(s) and all copies of them or any part of them to the SO on completion of the Works or termination of the Contract.

3
Care, protection and safety of the Works, the Site and Things

The Contractor is solely responsible for the care, protection and safety of the Works, the Site and all Things on the Site, and must:

(a) take all reasonable steps to make sure that any part of the Works or the Site which is or might be dangerous is properly secured and, where appropriate, illuminated; and

(b) keep the Site clean and tidy.

4
Damage to the Works or Things

(1) If any loss or damage is caused to the Works or to any Things on the Site (including any Things provided by the Authority) the Authority may, whatever the cause:

(a) require the Contractor to make it good; or

(b) (without prejudice to any other power to do so) terminate the Contract.

(2) If the Authority requires the Contractor to make good any such loss or damage, the Contractor must bear the cost of doing so, except that the Authority must pay him (as appropriate) the whole or a reasonable proportion of the cost of making good any loss or damage wholly or partly caused by:

(a) the neglect or default of a Servant of the Crown acting in the course of his official duties; or

(b) any person executing other work on behalf of the Authority under Condition 6; or

(c) any of the Accepted Risks.

(3) If the Authority terminates the Contract under this Condition, the Contractor shall only be entitled to be paid, in respect of the whole of the Contract:

(a) a reasonable proportion of the Price for any undamaged part of the Works; and

(b) the amount of any payment to which he would have been entitled under paragraph (2) above if the Contract had not been terminated and the Contractor had made good the loss or damage;

and the Contractor must repay any excess of any payments made under Condition 14.

5

Personal Injury and Loss of Property

(1) This Condition applies to any Personal Injury or Loss of Property (not falling within Condition 4) which arises in any way in connection with the performance or purported performance of the Contract.

(2) Subject to the following provisions of this Condition, the Contractor must:

(a) compensate the Crown for any such Loss of Property suffered by the Crown;

(b) indemnify the Crown and/or Servants of the Crown against any liability to anyone for any such Personal Injury or Loss of Property, and against all costs and expenses reasonably incurred in connection therewith;

(c) reimburse the Crown for the amount of any payment made to indemnify, in whole or in part, a Servant of the Crown against any such liability, costs or expenses; and

(d) reimburse the Crown for the amount of any payment made to a Servant of the Crown, whether under a Government Provision or otherwise, in connection with any such Loss of Property or Personal Injury suffered by him.

(3) **(a)** If the Contractor shows that any such Personal Injury or Loss of Property was wholly caused by the neglect or default of somebody other than himself or his sub-contractors or suppliers or his or their employees or agents or by any circumstances beyond his or their control, he will not be liable under this Condition.

(b) If the Contractor shows that any such Personal Injury or Loss of Property was partly so caused, any payment for which the Contractor would otherwise be liable under this Condition shall be reduced by a reasonable proportion to reflect the extent to which that neglect, default or circumstance contributed to it.

(4) **(a)** The Authority must notify the Contractor of any claim made in respect of any such Personal Injury or Loss of Property.

(b) If the Contractor admits that he is liable wholly to indemnify the Crown in respect of any such claim he, or if he so wishes his insurers, must (subject to sub-paragraphs (c) and (d) below) deal with or settle that claim.

(c) The Crown shall in any event deal with any such claim which involves a Government Provision or which is made by or against a Servant of the Crown, and sub-paragraph (b) above shall not apply to any such claim.

(d) If, when the Contractor or his insurers are dealing with any such claim, any matter arises which involves, or may involve, any privilege or special right of the Crown (including a matter relating to the discovery or production of documents) the Contractor or his insurers must consult the Authority before taking any further action on the matter and must obey the Authority's instructions on it; and if the Contractor or his insurers fail(s) to comply with this sub-paragraph, the Crown shall take over and deal with the claim, and if the Crown does take over the claim sub-paragraph (b) above shall cease to apply to it.

(5) If the Crown or a Servant of the Crown settles a claim in respect of any liability referred to in paragraph 2 (b) or (c) above, the amount of the settlement shall be regarded as correctly reflecting the liability, except insofar as the Contractor can show that that amount was not reasonable in all the circumstances.

6

Facilities for other work

The Authority may at any time execute other work (whether or not connected with the Works) on the Site, or engage another contractor to do so; and the Contractor must give reasonable facilities for that purpose.

7

Contractor to conform to regulations

Where the Works or any part of them are to be executed within a government establishment, the Contractor must comply with any rules and regulations of the establishment which are specified in the Contract.

8

Racial discrimination

The Contractor must not contravene the Race Relations Act 1976; and he must take all reasonable steps to ensure that his sub-contractors and suppliers, and his and their employees and agents, do not do so.

9 Admission to the Site and passes

(1) If the Authority or the SO gives the Contractor notice that anyone in particular or of a given description is not to be admitted to the Site, the Contractor must take all reasonable steps to prevent any such person being admitted and to ensure that any such person leaves the Site if he is already there; and the Contractor must replace any such person where appropriate.

(2) The Contractor must take any steps which the SO requires to prevent any alien who is not a citizen of a member state of the European Economic Community being admitted to the Site without the Authority's prior written permission.

(3) To the extent required from time to time by the SO or the Authority, the Contractor must provide the SO with:

(a) a list showing the name and address of everyone whom the Contractor wishes to be admitted to the Site and/or everyone else who is or may at any time be in any other way involved in the performance of the Contract, the capacity in which each person is or may be so involved and any other particulars required;

(b) satisfactory evidence as to the identity of each such person; and/or

(c) any other information about each such person, with supporting evidence, required.

(4) (a) Where the List of Contract Documents says that passes are required, the SO must (subject to satisfactory completion of clearance procedures) arrange for passes to be issued.

(b) Anyone who cannot produce a proper pass when required to by any appropriate Servant or agent of the Crown, or who contravenes any conditions on the basis of which a pass was issued, may be refused admission to the Site or required to leave it if he is already there.

(c) The Contractor must promptly return any pass if at any time the SO requires, or if the person for whom it was issued ceases to be involved in the performance of the Contract; and he must promptly return all passes on completion of the Works or termination of the Contract.

(5) The decision of the Authority, the SO or any such Servant or agent of the Crown as to whether any person is to be admitted to, or required to leave, the Site, or as to whether the Contractor has provided the information and evidence or taken the steps required by this Condition, shall be final and conclusive.

10 Photographs

The Contractor must not, without the Authority's prior written permission, take any photograph of the whole or any part of the Site, the Works or any Thing for Incorporation (whether on or off the Site); and he must also take all reasonable steps to prevent any person, other than the SO or any person authorised by him, from taking, publishing or otherwise circulating any such photograph without such permission.

11 Secrecy

The Contractor

(a) must not pass on any information obtained during or in connection with the performance of the Contract, except where necessary for the performance of the Contract or where authorised;

(b) must not contravene the Official Secrets Acts 1911 to 1939 (or, where appropriate, section 11 of the Atomic Energy Act 1946);

(c) must familiarise himself with those Statutory Provisions, and take all reasonable steps to ensure that his sub-contractors and suppliers, and his and their employees and agents, are familiar with them; and

(d) must take all reasonable steps to ensure that those people comply with paragraphs (a) and (b) above.

12

Defects appearing before the end of the Maintenance Period (only applicable if the List of Contract Documents says so)

(1) **(a)** If any defects in the Works arising out of the Contractor's neglect or default appear before the end of the Maintenance Period, the Contractor must make them good at his own cost.

(b) If the Contractor fails to make good any such defects, the Authority may get someone else to make them good, and the Contractor must pay the Authority for the cost of doing so.

(2) This Condition shall not affect any liability of the Contractor to pay damages in respect of any defects which appear after the end of the Maintenance Period.

13

SO's approval and Contractor's liability

The fact that the SO is satisfied with the Works or any part of them shall not affect the Contractor's liability under Condition 12 above, where it applies, or for damages.

14

Progress payments (only applicable if the List of Contract Documents says so)

(1) The Contractor may claim one third of the Price when one third of the Works has been completed, and another third of the Price when two thirds of the Works have been completed.

(2) **(a)** The Contractor must deliver his claims for payment under this Condition to the SO, who must arrange for payment if (and only if) he is satisfied that the required proportion of the Works has been satisfactorily executed.

(b) The Authority may deduct from the payment a reasonable proportion of any sum which the Contractor has agreed to pay for old materials to cover any such materials which he has already removed.

15

Final payment

(1) After completion of the Works, the Contractor must deliver a detailed account to the Department of the Environment at the address indicated on the order for work to proceed, or any other address required by the Authority.

(2) When the Contractor has delivered a proper account and the SO has certified that the Works have been satisfactorily completed the Authority must pay any outstanding part of the Price, less any outstanding part of any sum payable by the Contractor for old materials.

16

Termination of Contract

(1) The Authority may (without prejudice to any other right to terminate the Contract or to any claim for damages in respect of any breaches of the Contract) by notice terminate the Contract if:

(a) the SO gives notice to the Contractor, ordering him to rectify, reconstruct or replace any defective work or Things, or stating that work is being performed in an inefficient or otherwise improper manner, and the Contractor fails to comply with the requirements of the notice within seven days after the day of service;

(b) the Contractor fails to complete the Works on or before the Date for Completion or if he delays or suspends the execution of the Works so that he will, in the SO's opinion, be unable to complete them on or before that Date;

(c) the Contractor (or, where the Contractor is a partnership, any partner) is a company, and the company passes a resolution or the court makes an order that it shall be wound up, or if it makes an arrangement with its creditors or if a receiver or manager on behalf of a creditor is appointed, or if circumstances arise which entitle the court or a creditor to appoint a receiver or manager or which entitle the court to make a winding-up order;

(d) the Contractor (or, where the Contractor is a partnership, any partner) is an individual, and he at any time becomes bankrupt, or has a receiving order or administration order made against him or makes any composition or arrangement with or for the benefit of his creditors, or makes any conveyance or assignment for the benefit of his creditors, or purports to do so, or if in Scotland he becomes insolvent or notour bankrupt, or any application is made under any Statutory Provision relating to bankruptcy for sequestration of his estate, or a trust deed is granted by him for behoof of his creditors;

(e) the Contractor fails to comply with Condition 7, 9, 10 or 11, and the Authority (whose decision on this matter shall be final and conclusive) decides that failure is prejudicial to the interests of the State;

(f) the Contractor or anyone employed by him or acting on his behalf is found to have contravened the Prevention of Corruption Acts 1889 to 1916 in relation to this or any other contract with the Crown; or

(g) the Contractor is found to have broken the Rules about Confidentiality of Tenders.

(2) If the Contract is terminated under this Condition the Authority may either himself complete the Works, or engage any other contractor or contractors to do so, and recover from the Contractor the cost, if any, in excess of that which would have been payable under the Contract for completion.

17

Recovery of sums due from the Contractor

Any sum which is recoverable from or payable by the Contractor under the Contract may be deducted from or reduced by any sum(s) then due, or which may thereafter become due, to the Contractor under or in respect of the Contract or any other contract with the Crown.

18

Interpretation etc.

(1) The Glossary below shall apply for the interpretation of the Contract.

(2) The headings to these Conditions shall not affect their interpretation.

(3) Any reference in the Contract to any Statutory Provision includes any modification, re-enactment or replacement of it.

(4) If there is any discrepancy between these Conditions and the Specification(s) and/or the Drawing(s), these Conditions shall prevail.

(5) Any decision or action to be taken by the Authority under the Contract may be taken by any person authorised to act for him for that purpose and may be taken in such manner and on such evidence or information as he or such person thinks fit.

(6) Any notice to be given to either party under the Contract shall be in writing; and any notice to the Contractor which is sent by registered post or recorded delivery to the last known place of abode or business of the Contractor shall be deemed to have been served on the date when in the ordinary course of post it would have been delivered there.

(7) The proper law of the Contract shall be English law unless the Works are situated in Scotland when the Contract shall in all respects be construed and operate as a Scottish contract and shall be interpreted in accordance with Scots law.

GLOSSARY

In the Contract (unless the context otherwise requires) –

'the Accepted Risks' means –

(a) pressure waves caused by aircraft or other aerial devices whether travelling at sonic or supersonic speeds;

(b) ionising radiations or contamination by radioactivity from any nuclear fuel or from any nuclear waste from the combustion of nuclear fuel;

(c) the radioactive, toxic, explosive or other hazardous properties of any explosive nuclear assembly or nuclear component thereof; and

(d) war, invasion, act of foreign enemy, hostilities (whether or not war has been declared), civil war, rebellion, revolution, insurrection, or military or usurped power;

'the Authority' means the Secretary of State for the Environment;

'the Contract' means the written agreement concluded by the tender and acceptance, and all other documents referred to in them, including these Conditions, the Specification(s) and/or the Drawing(s) and any other documents or details mentioned or given in the List of Contract Documents;

'**the Contractor**' means the person(s) whose tender is accepted by the Authority and his or their legal personal representatives or permitted assigns;

'**the Crown**' includes the Authority;

'**the Date for Completion**' means the date specified, or the last day of the period specified, for the purpose in the List of Contract Documents (and where a period is specified, that period shall begin on the day after the day for commencement stated in the written order for work to proceed);

'**Government Provision**' means any Statutory Provision, warrant, order, scheme, regulations or conditions of service applicable to a Servant of the Crown providing for continuance of pay or for payment of sick pay, or any allowance to or for the benefit of Servants of the Crown, or their families or dependants, during or in respect of sickness, injury or disablement suffered by such Servants;

'**the List of Contract Documents**' means the list of contract documents on the tender form;

'**Loss of Property**' includes damage to property, loss of profits and loss of use;

'**the Maintenance Period**' means the maintenance period specified in the List of Contract Documents and shall begin on the day after the day on which the Works are satisfactorily completed as certified by the SO;

'**Personal Injury**' includes sickness and death;

'**the Price**' means the price tendered by the Contractor, and accepted by the Authority, for the execution of the Works;

'**Rules about Confidentiality of Tenders**' means the rules on the tender form concerning information and arrangements about tenders headed 'Confidentiality of tenders';

'**Servant of the Crown**' includes any person (and the personal representatives of any person) who was a servant of the Crown when any relevant Personal Injury or Loss of Property occurred, even if he has ceased to be such before any payment in respect of the Personal Injury or Loss of Property is made;

'**the Site**' means the land or place where the Works are to be executed and any other land or place provided by the Authority for or in connection with the execution of the Works;

'**the SO**' means the architect, engineer or surveyor (including any person acting for him) appointed for the time being by the Secretary of State for the Environment as superintending officer for the purposes of the Contract;

'**the Specification(s) and/or the Drawing(s)**' means the specification(s) and/or the drawing(s) mentioned in the List of Contract Documents;

'**Statutory Provision**' means any provision contained in or having effect under any enactment;

'**Things**' means Things for Incorporation and Things Not for Incorporation;

'**Thing for Incorporation**' means any thing for incorporation in the Works;

'**Thing Not for Incorporation**' means any thing provided for the execution of the Works other than a Thing for Incorporation;

'**VAT**' means value added tax within the meaning of the Value Added Tax Act 1983;

'**the Works**' means the works described in the Specification(s) and/or the Drawing(s).

Printed in the UK for HMSO
Dd 738721 C100 9/85